Uncommon Prayer

Uncommon Prayer

Kimberly Johnson

POEMS

A Karen & Michael Braziller Book
PERSEA BOOKS / NEW YORK

Persea Books, Inc.
277 Broadway
New York, NY 10007

Library of Congress Cataloging-in-Publication Data
        Library of Congress Cataloging-in-Publication Data
Johnson, Kimberly, 1971—
[Poems. Selections]
Uncommon prayer : poems / Kimberly Johnson.—First edition.
        pages ; cm
"A Karen & Michael Braziller book."
ISBN 978-0-89255-447-8 (original trade pbk. : alk. paper)
I. Title.
PS3610.O36A6 2014
811'.6—dc23
                    2014018151

First edition
Printed in the United States of America
Designed by Rita Lascaro

For Jay Hopler, uncommon answer

CONTENTS

III. *Siege Psalter*

Man builds a Cathedrall the better to hear him selfe.

—CHRISTOPHER WREN

*But when men saye Matins and Evensong
privatelye, they maye saie the same in any language
that they themselves do understande.*

—1549 *BOOK OF COMMON PRAYER*

I.

Book of Hours

MATINS FOR THE LAST FROST

Patient in their dark hibernacle
wait the twinned lobes of the tulip bulb
hanging like a semicolon
in the endless sentence of winter;
not yet the green shaft rips the paper tunic
in its upward thrust, not yet knifes its tip
through the topsoil, the stalk aspiring
up to a swelling of petals, pale
bud pursed and then loosened, deepening
to red and unsealing itself sash by sash,
a leggy dishabille in lipstick.

Somewhere on the other side of town
some bells begin to raise their brazen;
everything is about to change—

BLANKS

The sun rolls up like jackpot,
the thousand blinding coins of it spilling
across my windshield's dustdapple.
Glory be: my lucky day, flush and prime
as a fresh dime, as if the world been spitshined.
The asphalt ahead's gleamed to a high glare
and I play my pedal past the red line, and faster.
Must be what faith feels like, to drive believing
in the persistence of highway lines
whose white paint's whitened to a wide white field,
to glimpse in swift periphery and guess
you've passed a reststop's spare oasis,
to catch the flicker of a cactus shadow
as a signpost toward some providential end.
If on such a visionary road
I should see the world's material scroll
back to show whatever lies behind
who would blame me? Who'd blame if I sublimed
each raw thing into a revelation—
the big-rig flipping its rockchip stigmata,
the naugahyde peeling an unction
from my thigh. But no. Faith's for the sucker
whose luck's run out. Faith is for the fear
that sometimes you get cherries, and sometimes
you pull the handle and it comes up blanks.

THREE LAUDS

1.

Praise to the joshua, that awkward knob
of spikes, how they jostle the horizon
like a desert of elbows.

2.

Praise say we who are assembled here
at this reststop

            to this reststop, its stainless
washroom basin the last for ninety miles.
Praise to the freshwater spigot, the gravel
path winding along and away
from the asphalt to the only tree in sight.
An ash, shading a pool of grass.

3.

Praise to the bareknuckle sun, whose glory
is to stun us with our own precariousness.
So much light and heat here, where the car-top
sears the thumbprint from the thumb, and the throat's
reservoirs parch. Praise, for praise is a punchback,
in the song-shimmered air a shadow the shape of the sun.

Book of Hours

A pentecost of bloom: all the furred tongues
awag in the iris patch, windrush through the fireflower.
To what wonders they may testify
I don't know; my earthy idiom hears as noise the hiss
of sweet alyssum and the bees' melisma.
Shouldn't that be enough?—but I fidget
around the garden like a wasp for nectar,
greedy, antic, spoiling for the ruin
of meaning. One long morning I looked thus
at inkwork on trussed vellum, a gospel
in cochineal and verdigris, gold leaf
haloing the majuscule. The manuscript
twined a black briar stem and barb from margin
to margin. No untangling that liturgy,
no telling the prayers in its glittering pigments.
Yet I adored each page, and bent to stare
so low that my lips touched the serif
of an illuminated T. I left
the archive chrismed with turmeric—,
until, in the sudden rain, all that I kept
of that book washed from me. The spirit's
a terse mutter to the flesh's aria, but I'll forget
today's ecstasies when the wind dies,
forget their honeyed buzz when the bees hive up
for evening. Against the stillness of that fast-
approaching, anaesthetic dark
I nuzzle the humblest buds to my chin, dust
the shyest pistils across my wrist,
and when too noiselessly their petals brush

my ear, I will declare them from my very lungs
and I will mouth the wind back upon itself:
Paperwhite. Paperwhite. Incarnadine.

THE TRUMPETVINE CLARIONS TO THE HONEYBEES

Another season on beautiful fire.
Another hummingbird needles the bloom-
swung branches of my plum tree, his bleeding
heart of feathers beating at such speed
it seems unbeating, and in the sun's unclouding
the tanager's intemperate plumage
flickers at the tree's equator. This spring
came on too much like dawn, all at once
with too much noise and color—the sun
so bright the dead are getting jumpy,
upkindling like pasqueflowers
when the green current starts to tendril
through the deciduous flesh of them. So fierce
these early-season stirrings that I envy
them, the dead, whose ardor is dispersed
and muted by the intermediary soil:
my senses sway all the way down to the bone
even on dull-lighted days, but O!— spring ignites
that fuse which, as it five-alarms up
the middle of me, would consume those blooms,
the flash-feathered tanager, the plumstained
hummingbird, his luscious and breakneck heart,
the very sun. Elemental, irresistible,
spring thrusts its coal into my mouth,
and I burn like judgment day.

NONESUCH

Not this: you the urge and I the page.
Not this: you the harrow, blades sharp
to turn the fallow field of me. Not the wheel
that turning winds the carded wool of me.
Not you the pick and I the Rickenbacker
cherryneck with the humbucker pickups.
Not you the piston whose combusted thrust
shoves the rod that drives my crankshaft.
Not I the vehicle, not I the sign
and you the substance, you the blessed body
absent and sublime and I your accident.
Not though we both were nothing thereby.
You are not my _____.   I am not your sign.

CREPUSCULAR

What a drubbing this sundown!—its gloom
hunting out my sorest remorses
to bludgeon me with. That's what the light does
in autumn, slanting southward and brownly
between the hunched houses of the neighborhood.
It falls against the sidewalk like a slab
of meat, like a mugging the passersby pass by.
The churchbells bang hollow vespers.
Is there any sound more forsaken
than the rainbird smack across the spent grass?
Yes.   The ignition jump of a car
heading anywhere, taillights red
as the rubber stamp on a divorce decree,
its diminishing rev a metaphor
for the failure of metaphor. The car
is a car leaving, and then left.

Big Finish

Now that the last shaft of sunset has collapsed
into that rubble of cloud, let's dust off
and see how bright the stars are, the disclosed
vault spinning like a discoball been drilled
smack into Polaris. My oracle's
a bullhorn for the endtimes, portending
wars and rumors of wars in the stars' course
headlong through the heavens. And even though
the astrophysicists as in chorus
to the oracle declare that all this sparkle,
every spectacular atom of it,
is a death, the expired light of bodies
that have burned themselves down to nothing,
yet they are so bright and shimmery,
and to shimmy seems their light to me,
sequins tilting into a spotlight.
Don't they move like jubilation on their wheel?
And don't they flash with brash abandon?
And if finally they should quit their spheres
and fall upon us, their apocalypse
will surely seem a shower not of wormwood
but confetti, gleeful streaking
down the sackcloth dark to pronounce our doom.
A wop bop a loo-bop, a wop-bam-boom.

A Nocturnall Upon Saint Chuck Yeager's Day

              Here comes that sonic boom
thumping at the chest like a kickdrum
the first and final beat of a tune called
Too Late. Ever too late the event
reveals its narrative to the sense
ever too slow on the uptake,
ever life hurtles heartbreak to heartbreak
while I rattle around in its mach-cone
trying to work out the ever-aftermath.

*

To the palm that rests atop the trembling
diaphragm, not to calm but to confirm
the body's record, all this shock and roar
is a comfort. After such rough cleavings—
molecule from molecule, the sound shorn
back from the air and stacked upon itself—
there should be noise. There should be a bombblast
bellknocking bonejar of noise, a jolt
to all wavelengths, a tremor through the pavement
tripping car-alarms and dog-howls to the proof
that something happened.

*

Something happened. Something wider than the sky
got broken, something faster than a word
arrowed into it, and that damned and blessed
sonic boom is rolling on past me
                drumming up the next dirge
                by the time I know to mourn
whatever it was.

REQUIEM

O, to be still. To bury in winter this clamorous
flesh, howling need from its first breath. To recover
from mothballs the muffler, the flannel, the consolation
of moonboots. Who would not wish for such stillness?
But even when the snow recovers the fields
and winds around the sky a white sheet,
and I am wound to the ears in muffling,
still the brain jangles in its pan
like a single alms-penny. Poor brain. Its hungers
make the body an amateur. It thinks
that if it studies the almanac's seasonal assurances,
The Weather Channel and the hard promise of seed
catalogues, the field guides and the dictionary
with its litany of disappointments, the desperate order
of the Book of Hours, the common prayers and private,
all the old elegies, each one a plea
to the loud and unresponsive night
it will understand longing.
                    —Which is to say, grief.

VIGIL

The time of miracles is past, as the stars
do not declare in their slow shrug over
the shot-bulb dark of the back lot
of the Second Universalist Church. What
did I think I'd see? An omen of lyrids?
The aurora borealis winging
like a wurlitzer annunciation?
I am too late, and too far declined
from true north for visitations,
and my great symbolic stars
mean *hydrogen*, mean *gravity*, mean *mass*.
The church windows are low and dark, no belfry
to tell the hours but the fitful buzz
of a bug-zapper, the windknock of apples
untimely onto roofs. Some bird chatters something
I can't make out. In all the watches
of the night, all the world's objects crowd
around me, all flaunting their gorgeous
opaque. Miraculous unknowable:
is this what I've been watching for?

A Benediction: On the Tulpenwoede of Seventeenth-Century Holland

Blessed be the disease, the virus subtle
plunging to the heart of every bulb
to break as streaks and flames through the conservatory,
waxy petals freaked with frantic pinks
and periwinkles. Blessed be the rankle
that stains its mosaic cell to cell,
forcing through each blowsy stem-heavy bloom
color undreamed by the feyest confectioner
until the very air seems motley. Blessed
the collectors infected by desire:
how they want; how they lick their lips
as if they would devour at the bud
each sudden new original
and its exponential next; how they settle
for a name that they can hold between the teeth,
biting down against this infinite
variety. And blessed, O blessed
all those names, all the neat rows of them
in the ledger a dear anthology
of failures: the *Semper Fidelis*
subsides to the *Fidelis* in a season,
the *Volition* evolves into the *Volitant*.
Blessed that rage to corner the rarest cultivar,
to press tight as in a book each beauty
made beautiful by its not enduring.
Bookkeeper, I am your daughter, believing
that by loving I could hold what I loved,
forgetting that I loved because I couldn't.

II.

Uncommon Prayers

ORANGE TREE

My everlasting sun!
—Hung like tungsten fruit from the ceiling vault

Of the orangerie, my ever-clement sky.
Let December crash its petals at the glass,

Let January clench the world down
To its heartwood, let March savage like hatchets

Like cutworms   like budmites   like rootrot
Like the end of possibility,

I will fan my laze-laden branches
In the precise sighs of the central air.

Let God drop like a heatlamp from his rafters
And scorch the heart to its pith, I will plump

My boughs, and preen, and give thanks
For my splendid self. See how the known world depends

On my knowing it, how my slender shadow
Seems to fall upon all things? The orangerie wall

Fills with the shape of me: my brainstem trunk,
My bravery of leaves in their evergreen hemispheres,

My branches hung with the ripening weight
Of my best offspring, that luscious and heavy O

For oblivion.

APPLE TREE

I winter too well. My seventh spring
And still no bloom beguiles upon my boughs.

The plum blossoms primp and blandish,
The pear tree lavishes itself in white

But leaf-lush I'm this bounteous, greenest waste.
My seventh June finds me fruitless again

While the sweet cherries swell, the apricots
Apricate. Where is the orchardman's

Pocketknife?—whose flashed passage through my bast
May blister a fruit-spur to flower,

Spring flair for next year's harvest. *O bless me*
Not with inconsequential beauty . . .

It's the prayer we all whisper:
The plum tree dropping birdpocked, rotten

Half-prunes all through August, the pulped cherries
On their branches browning to fall,

And through the grove lugging his unlovely limbs
The orchardman with the knife his flower.

Bug-zapper

Come, flame-moth. Come, feathered thornwing,
Darkling beetle and Asian lady, and come,

O nightwasp. Swift through the soft air fly
To where I hang allurement.

I am caged moon! I am firefly phosphorescence
Slow-gracing to the rooftree! I am anything

But this low-watt hum, this dim fluorescent sham
Slung rusting from the rain gutter,

Cord rubbed raw to the next rain's
Sputter, short-out, and dark. When you arc

From the ether to my electrical field,
I am ethereal, something worth

Steering for. And if, when you reach me,
You should vaporize,   —Well,

That's what we celestials do: we firework;
We meteor in streaks, lit up

Like a house afire, like bad wiring
On dry-rot wood. My brief lovelies,

Let us spark while we can.
I feel a hard rain coming on.

PITBULL

You slow thing,
You with your superfluous yips,

What can you suppose I want from you?
My instinct feeds me; I can tooth-and-claw

Any bone to brightness, I lick the sockets
Of the air to track my next hunger.

But you who of your urges make ideas
Can't guess why I break from your steadfast

And dull pettings for the first ripe bitch I smell,
My magnificent flanks flexing toward her

As you spindle along far behind;
Why sniffing her asshole wags the stars;

Or why I tongue and tongue a sore
To keep it raw and salty. My next hunger

Is me: the rare, incarnate meat of me.
O frail, O small, if you want me

To love you, take off your muzzle
Of words and fang this pig's ear of a world,

Your mouth, for once, filled only with your teeth.

WRECKINGBALL

With what stern determination I love
That wall!—: its red height so certain I must

Fling myself at it, an erratic
Embarrassment of a fling, chain-wobbling

Through my drunk parabola to kiss
The brick. Can I help it that I kiss

With all my force? Nuzzled
To dust, all my beloveds must wish

To have gone unregarded. What do
I wish for? *The end of love.*

METRONOME

I'm done with this buck and wing, the shuck and jive
Of marking time for you. A spring sprung,

A gear-catch at each lefthand lurch, and zing!—
I've a hitch in my get-along. I lopside

Like a kite ride, struggle upright from the downswing,
My hammer-hand dragging in the end-zone:

I am become an undependulum.
Isn't this bliss, this shift from Old Reliable

To Whiplash Skip in a quicker-than-a-tick?
For so long I have so longed not to steady you,

Steady your tune, bury my backbeat in the background.
Let the town talk about my late stroke, scold

That I put the *sin* in *syncopate*. I'll take
My limp any time over your well-tempoed

Clever in the key of never again. And when
I'm left to hap my own hazard, useless in my slap

And dash, trash as trashtalk, I'll hang
My long left and shrug *At least I'm loud.*

ORBWEAVER

Fie I say to the knitting needles, fie
On their knotted purls, on the pliant loops

Of the crochet hook. Fie on macramé,
The embroiderer's gaudy floss, and fie

On all those green Minervas, each one shuttling
The warp of her tragedy line by line

Until the last picturesque thread pulls tight.
That's the trouble with art, how it aspires

To have been made: the throwpillow's
Cross-stitched *price above rubies* never frays

Into subclauses; on the tapestry
The woman waits forever at the seaward window,

Her lachrymal faith never unraveling
To resignation, to rage, to the day

She shucks the sackcloth, unpins her hair,
And bulldozes the porticoes down.

My spinnerets are honest: when I dragline
My aminos across the loom of sky,

The pattern grows more perfect in its unmaking—
The websilver franticked in tangles,

The spokes thrashed to snips. I would scorn
A thousand squares of finest linen

For one rag with a bulb of blood at its heart.
How lifelike the design that starts in assurance

And ends with a corpse. How providential.

CORPSE-FLOWER (*Amorphophallus titanum*)

This morning's hothouse: a pornography.
All my darlings pressing up to watch

My fan-dance, velvet spathe flourishing
Open to my hidden plush. I will peel down

To my inmost creases for you, and your camera
Will snap and whine, but we both know

You're not after some glossy shot
For your desktop botanical. What you want

You can't film: the meat-wet stench
Of my inflorescence, ruined sweet

Like a carcass heat-rotting in the compost heap.
You throb at my illicit coupling

Of lily-purple with putrid, at how at my shift
Into fullest splendor I am most refulgent-foul.

But the carrion bugs and fleshflies call me
Beautiful, and race to kiss my fleeting bloom

And lard their chops with pollen, and swoon
Under the smell of *just proportion:*

Of what should beauty smell
If not of death, whose flower it is?

CATAPULT

Knock back the catch on the spooled cord, and let fly!
Skyward my blithe *port de bras*, and skyward flings

Anything you give me: flaming haybales,
Boulders, wet mounds of dung, groundling stuff

Which airborne turns unearthly beauty, unbodied grace
For which the battlement's too mean a target.

See how, shot, that clatter of tacks glints
Like stars above the bonfires, how that vat of rendered fat

Anoints the fortress walls with burning.
See how the corpses of the hostile dead

Hang angelic in the middle air. And how, angelic,
They fall, as if hungering for the earth

And its sweet demolishings. *Holy the fall.*
I hymn it with my arm.

WASP

My name is Legion, and my sisters' name
Is Legion. When we awoke beneath the silkscreen

Of spring sunlight through the pines, we hummed
Confusion, and the hum resounding

Cell to cell assumed the shape of the vespiary.
It meant *communion*. We shook our new wings

And set out to expand our echo chamber.
More sound we buzzed one to another

As we milled the rotten stump, *More*
Scraping off fibers of fencepost, and, fitting

The pulp into place with our spit, we murmured
To hatchlings *More sound* summer-long. Now as the evening star

Nests like a queen, we swarm through the vestibule
Into the vault, and whisper. The paper

Whispers back. It is our stay against the wide,
Illegible night. It is our book of common prayer.

The Lord God Bird (*Campephilus principalis*)

Knock-knock on the cracked bark of the sweet gum,
And *knock-knock* in echo through cypresses

Swamp-sunk to their bent knees. The punchline
Is that there's no punchline, only silence

Closing like a cloud around the place
Wherefrom you thought you heard me call.

You can yoo-hoo your heart out, I will hidden hold
My operatic plumage, fold wings

Over my ivory and my wound-red crown.
I will wind so tight myself in feather and fern

That you who've tramped years through this tract with your Kodaks,
Your boom-mike humming dumbly reel to reel,

Must take heavy up the bureaucratic pen
And scratch the fatal asterisk to my name.

Then when you've closed your logbook, and loaded up
Your johnboat with all those unconsoling tools,

Then will I swoop the Spanish moss, my white wingtips
Aflash in the canopy like the world's last morning,

And jaw my tinhorn squawk from trunk to trunk.
It's a trick I picked up from the grubs

Pathing the fat phloem far beneath the bark,
For whose love my bill evolved its ivory curve,

My lash-flicking tongue its barb:
If I made myself easy to be found,

Why would you look?

Cowpunch

Unhobble your hardscrabble horses, soul—
The night before us is steep and long,

And the steers won't drive themselves. They moan
In the gloaming, and clack horns

One to another's as to the comfort
Of fenceposts. Their nerves are barbed wire.

Footsore and far from pasture, we fret
A course across the endless range, the sage flats

A gray disorientation
Of spooks and noise to all horizons.

I with my whistle, my whipcrack
Consistency, am their only known thing,

And they will follow me anywhere:
To the hilltop, the feedlot, the bolt gun's

Red floor. The wind is picking up,
Trawling its weather; snow will hard fall

Like a heavy body and shove the dawn back down,
And if we, frostburnt, snowblind, shoulder

Through the storm to find our destination
It will kill us. Soul, I will follow you anywhere.

III.

Siege Psalter

Engine against th' Almighty...
—GEORGE HERBERT, "PRAYER (I)"

Alpha

As in *top dog*. Make that *top god*. Because you are nothing if not fond of wordplay, framing your absolutes in paradox and parable. The Word took Flesh, the Flesh took questions *and answered them nothing*, the Logos took silent, a perfect anagram of speech. Thus in your element I hound you, like a dogfighter made reckless by my losses, my rage an imperfect anagram of *grace*. Open thou my chops, O Lord, that I may howl your praise.

Bravo

The psalmists knew how to begin: by buttering up. *Who is like God?* Or *How excellent is thy name!* I will sing a new song unto the Lord, because my old songs got me nowhere. I need a song with legs, a rock song for the ages, to make the stadium leap with affirmation. The stadium loves to leap into the arclights, loves to wave its hands and tiny fires as if they were essential to the song, and loves to sing along. *Love me! Love me!* sing we all together, *for thy name's sake.*

Charlie

A new song. A carol, say, to constancy—not the Northstar's stubborn pivot, boring nightlong through the pole, but the modest steadfastness of the Big Dipper. Draw a line across its basin star to star and then beyond the constellation till you find, near-invisible, true North. Selfless gesture, at every hour to point and point away to some obscure and ever-fixèd mark, to be prized for pure devotion, for how it bears the gaze away . . . Isn't that how it is, in love as in war: someone gets to pull the wagon, and someone, girding his smallness in glittering mail, gets to be Charlemagne.

Delta

When thundering through the heavens I hear the B-2 Stealth Bomber—its elusive grace as it banks trailing fractals from its skin, its clandestine maneuvers, its trinitarian aerodynamism—I think of God. Dropping what ordnance I cannot tell, a fusillade unseen from where I cannot tell, kilotons to knock me to confusion. O Stealth Bomber, intermediary for the illegible, plead for me now in the hour of my whatever.

Echo

We'd make a legendary pair: you love the sound of your own voice, and I have to have the last word. But I'm no nymph pleading in perfect refrain, no ping for the smug submariner. Insubordinate, I embellish your cadence call; I run your reverb through my wah-wah, turn all your periods to colons; I slant, if I rhyme at all. I am here, in this deviance, and I am trying to help you find me. As if you were trying to find me.

Foxtrot

A new song, a new step. From the foxholes of the Great War the soldiers staggered into commissariat hotels, R&R illusions at the fringes of the front. The patriotic girls waited in their dancing shoes to shimmer through the newest-fangled *slow-slow-quick-quick*, because there wasn't any time to waltz. There never is. We bang into one another, tangle up and try to time our lurches to the timbrel and harp, to give them a shape that is comely and pleasing to make us forget for a moment the trenches and the grand historic sweep of hurt. Selah.

Golf

Glory be to God for bungled things, for the early frost, the miscarriage, the land mine sunk forgotten in the wheatfield, the liger. For all things marred and misbegotten, praise Him— hamfisted, hamstrung, and never else so like us. So comforting a kinship that we hymn it constantly: *"God!"* at the carpenter's hammered thumb, *"O God!"* at the failed marriage, *"God damn!"* on the fourteenth green. The chorus amens; cue the responsory:

Versicle: Why in lightning should you hold up a one iron?
Antiphon: Because not even God can hit a one iron.

Hotel

How hospitable these hired rooms! Their square corners and the assurance thereof, their efficiency! Here is the room in which we first met, years ago, you playing the victim and me on my knees. Here is the room where, Love, you invited me to recline upon the cushions and taste, a night unlike all the other nights. Here is the room where you stand with your knives to prepare a table before me in the presence of mine enemies. My dear host, dear hospitaller, all your rooms have enemies, and all are a sacrifice to leave. In my solitude are many mansions.

India

Having smacked down the Bactrian satrapies, Alexander dragged his armies eastward: over the Hindu Kush, through defiant foothills, against sickness and mutiny and the unprovisionable mass of his battalions to the great river's golden sands. So hungered he for the known world that he impious razed a hemisphere to possess its wreckage. Lucky, lucky world, to be so fiercely wanted.

Juliet

The girl knows drama, waking spotlit from her death with
the silver flask of cordial clutched inside her flounces to find
her husband cold and responseless. Even he was taken in by
her performance. What left to do but pray?— not to the God
who crossed their stars but to that other steely cordial. She's
sheathing her hope beneath her heart. She knows her role.

Kilo

Run twenty-six miles in armor to report the battle's outcome
and they'll name a race after you. Turn up the prattle of AM
gospel radio and all the lights in the house to counterweight
the long, long, lonely evening and the village averts itself,
clenches its very breastplate against your endurance. But O,
how the heart flouts our measure, runs too long past its limits,
its calculus of love and despair as refractory and unspeakable
as a bomb.

Lima

Come on, conquistador. Go down to my southernmost ports and see what gold awaits you. Give me your tongue and I will cleave unto it. I will overthrow my oracles to serve you. I will forget my original name and take yours. But if I ever forget you, my forgetful Love, *let my right hand forget her cunning.*

Mike

Is this thing on?

 And by *this thing* I mean *your heart*. At my least whisper it should shudder and surge in its die-cast shell, throbbing voltage into kilohertz. Are your works out of whack, did you blow a fuse?—To my boldest showstoppers no applause but static fuzz and the damp hum of my cranium. Have you heard the one about the _____? What do you get when you cross a _____? And here's one I'm just learning: *Knock-knock. Knock-knock. Knock-knock. Knock-knock. Knock-knock.*

Thank you, you're a swell audience. I'll be here my whole life.

November

Thirty days hath &c., but this one feels like forever, leaves taking their final separation from the limbs that long have loved them. Does the leaf strain beyond its petiole's strength, or does the branch at last let go? What an agony, to watch it happen again and again, until the yard is filled with summer's resignations. The light is crisp. A warm wind moves in the trees, stirring up a thousand golden swivels. It's enough to make you pray for winter.

Oscar

I'd like to thank my Agent Orange, whose soft and subtle fall shocked the foliage from my trees. No slow deforestation to prolong regret but the sudden candor of ruined boughs, pale and awkward in the nitrogen light. I like them better this way, the trees, brusque and intolerant of rhapsodies. Autumn's languishments are too lavish to be trusted, too artfully tragic, mugging like hell to distract us from all the rot.

Papa

Pack another dress in the hope chest, girlie. Three of them now, silking whitely into one another's folds: christening, confirmation, bridal. Each worn like a white flag; each outgrown. Which one did I wear when I took your name?—I can't keep them straight, all those dresses and names. My mister, my master, my man among men, I'm divesting, undressing down to the one that fits me best: *Never Good Enough*.

Quebec

You say *strait* and *narrows*, and I say *the roughest crossing my poor bark has ever tried*. No clemency at these latitudes—strafing headwind, headland barely seen for all the spray. Finally at promised landfall, no welcoming party: the permafrost echoes the remote vespers of Notre-Dame-des-Victoires. In the weather's shrill bombardment, I must have misheard you. I thought you said *I do*. You said *adieu*.

Romeo

Beneath the balcony, all swoon and swashbuckle. But when swords get drawn how soft his valor's steel, how speedy sped.

Sierra

When I sang *Ain't no mountain high 'nough/ Ain't no valley low 'nough*, I didn't know you'd take me at my word. I didn't know I'd find myself bivouacked on barren ground, a thousand miles behind me trudged, a thousand more to hike, the water scarce, the chiggers fierce, and everything ashimmer with illusions. I'm marching for that patch of green asplash at the horizon, where I'm certain you await me with soft linens and peeled grapes. The ridgeline juts above it like a saw, the kind that cuts a woman in half.

Tango

It takes two. Two to tangle. Two to gaze moon-eyed, to break into conversation. To sound the verse and antiphon. Two to hang a picture level. Two to screw in a light bulb, if one of them's a joker. It takes two to fracas, two to fuck. It takes two for transgression, two for atonement, two to hang around and talk this day of paradise. Two for prayer, and two for the prayer denied. But it only takes one to give up.

Uniform

Let's swallow hard and review the album. See the bridegroom dressed to perfection. See the bride adorned in her whitest finery. We shine right up to swear one flesh, one heart, one mind, the flashbulbs popping at our certainty. Which *cleave* did we promise at that day's altar? We should have sworn over the busted sewer pipe, or sleepless with a sick baby, or when the arguments turned bitter, or after I had lied. A vow's only as strong as its odds of breaking.

Victor

That long love whose bannered bravery flushed my brow has slunk back to my heart. My new flag semaphores *surrender*. Like the rose that gives over its damask to snow. Like the cloud that clings to light at the western edge, red as with exertion, until the sun at last withdraws and leaves it small and pale against the wide, dark sky.

Whiskey

Good God, I need a drink. I've been talking me hoarse, rehearsing full-throated my love's ferment. I pled into silence *As the heart panteth after the water brooks, so panteth my soul after thee.* O Water of Life, fill me up; make me your shotglass, your hipflask, my most hollow crannies brimming with you. Let me guzzle away the persistent, insatiate, maculate me of me.

X-ray

On the plate, my bones articulate their curves and sockets, pale blue against the black of my flesh. The skull's grim smile, the phalanges fanned across the sternum in a theatrical gesture of surprise, of romance. How intact I appear. I've counted the ribs a hundred times, and the number's even. Where's the original, the one that made me a collector's item? Burnt up, I suppose—one of the thousand private holocausts when the world passes through us and blasts our shades against the nearest wall.

Yankee

Farewell to the carillon whose golden hours belled through the cathedral's corset of vaults and over the tidy, empty house, the careful garden. I've left its exaltations far behind, my fine designs fallen before a more manifest destiny. In this new-found eden of trees, we keep slapdash time: around prime the bees lick the honeysuckle, the cock throats his raw aubade; for compline the doves murmur a serenade; and midnights no one sleeps for the cuckoo's constant racket in the understory. The wilderness keeps its sly and mysterious offices, a liturgy I'm trying to learn. I keep my whistle wet. I've taken off my wedding band. I'm letting my hair grow long.

Zulu

The compass; the antique dictionaries; the telescopic array; the atomic tick of meridian time: my first mistake was to believe that by sounding the furthest measures I might recover what was lost. The joke's on me. In the beginning was the originary split: heaven and earth irreconciled. So everything is born to loss. So every word is *grief*.

Outside, in the fundamental night, stars struggle up from the east. The clockhands struggle to the vertical hour. Somewhere, on the other side of the world, the sun is rising.

NOTES

"Book of Hours" is for Riley Lorimer.

"A Nocturnall...": Pilot Chuck Yeager broke the sound barrier in the experimental Bell X1 on October 14, 1947.

"Tulpenwoede," or *tulip mania*, is one of the Dutch names given to the market chaos that resulted from tulip speculation during the 1630s, in which prices for tulip bulbs reached exorbitant heights and then suddenly collapsed. The spectacular variety of these plants was produced as a result of the bulbs' being infected with a tulip mosaic virus. Infected bulbs make for rare (and therefore valuable, in a collector's market) strains of color patterning, because the pattern is passed only through offsets of the infected bulb.

"The Lord God Bird" is a common name for the ivory-billed woodpecker (*Campephilus principalis*). The largest woodpecker species in the world, its habitat spread throughout the swamps and pine forests of the American southeast. It was declared extinct in the 1920s, until a pair was spotted in Florida some years later. It has been presumed extinct a few times since then; each time a rare and tantalizing sighting—the sightings sometimes decades apart—has suggested that at least one bird remains. The current status of the species remains under debate.

"Golf" concludes with a quip attributed to American golfer Lee Trevino.

"Papa" owes its life to Kristen Eliason and Sarah Jenkins.

"Sierra" quotes lines written by Nickolas Ashford & Valerie Simpson, and recorded by Marvin Gaye and Tammi Terrill in 1967.

ACKNOWLEDGMENTS

Grateful recognition is due to the following publications, in which some of these poems, occasionally in different form, first appeared:

> *Barn Owl Review, Black Market Review, Connotation Press: An Online Artifact, Fence, Gulf Coast, The Hudson Review, Indiana Review, Lake Effect, Literary Imagination, Lo-Ball, Memorious, The Missouri Review, New England Review, New South, The New Yorker, Ploughshares, Plume, Poetry International, Slate*

I am indebted to those friends who read poems in this collection, and to Jay Hopler and Josh Bell for reading the whole thing. As ever, I appreciate the careful ministrations of my editor at Persea Books, Gabe Fried, and acknowledge with gratitude the enduring encouragement of Karen Braziller and Michael Braziller.

This book was completed with the generous support of a Fellowship from the John Simon Guggenheim Memorial Foundation.